I0468938

Merry-Go-Round

Adult Coloring Book

The Creativity Tree

Copyright April 2016

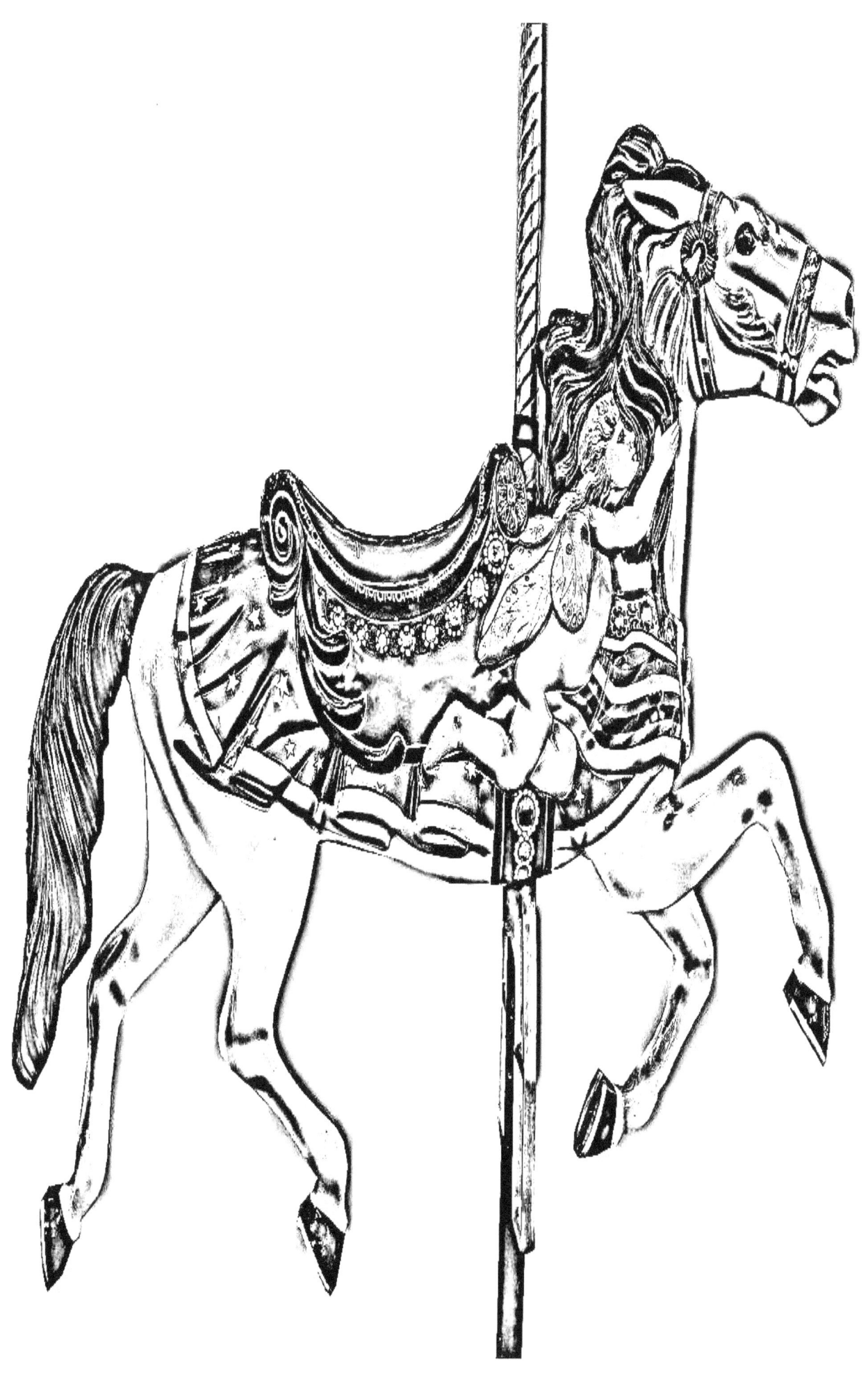

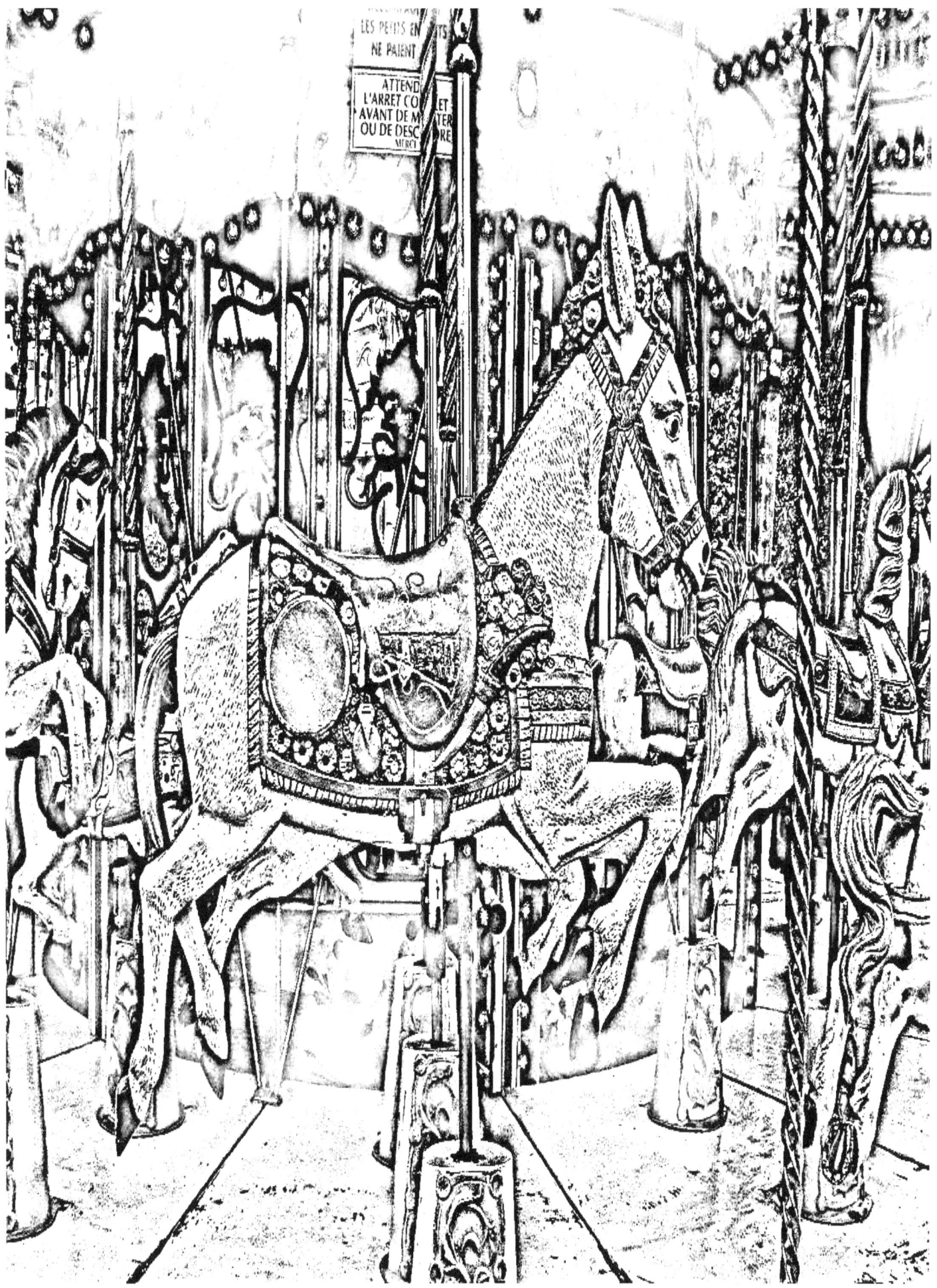

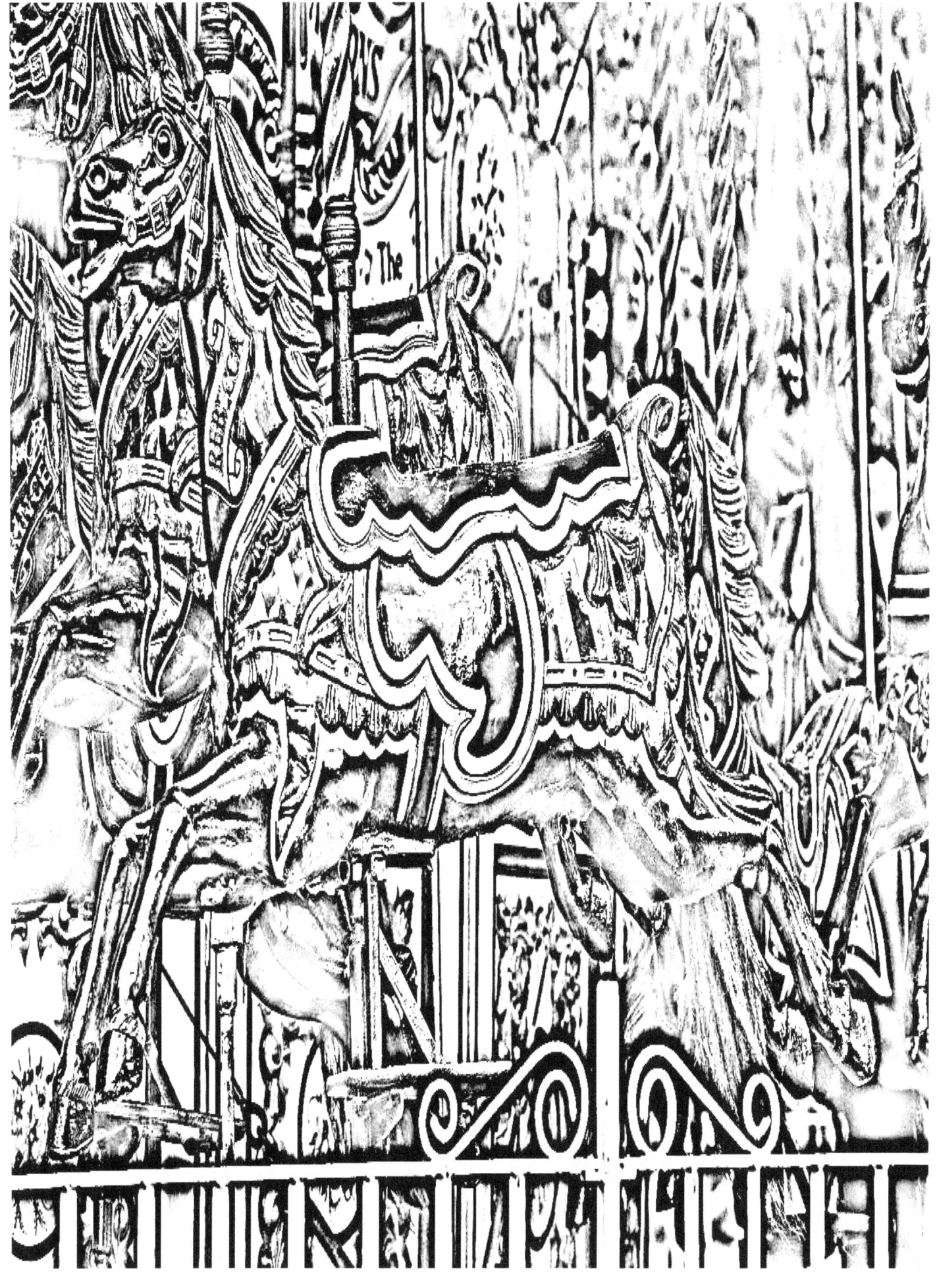

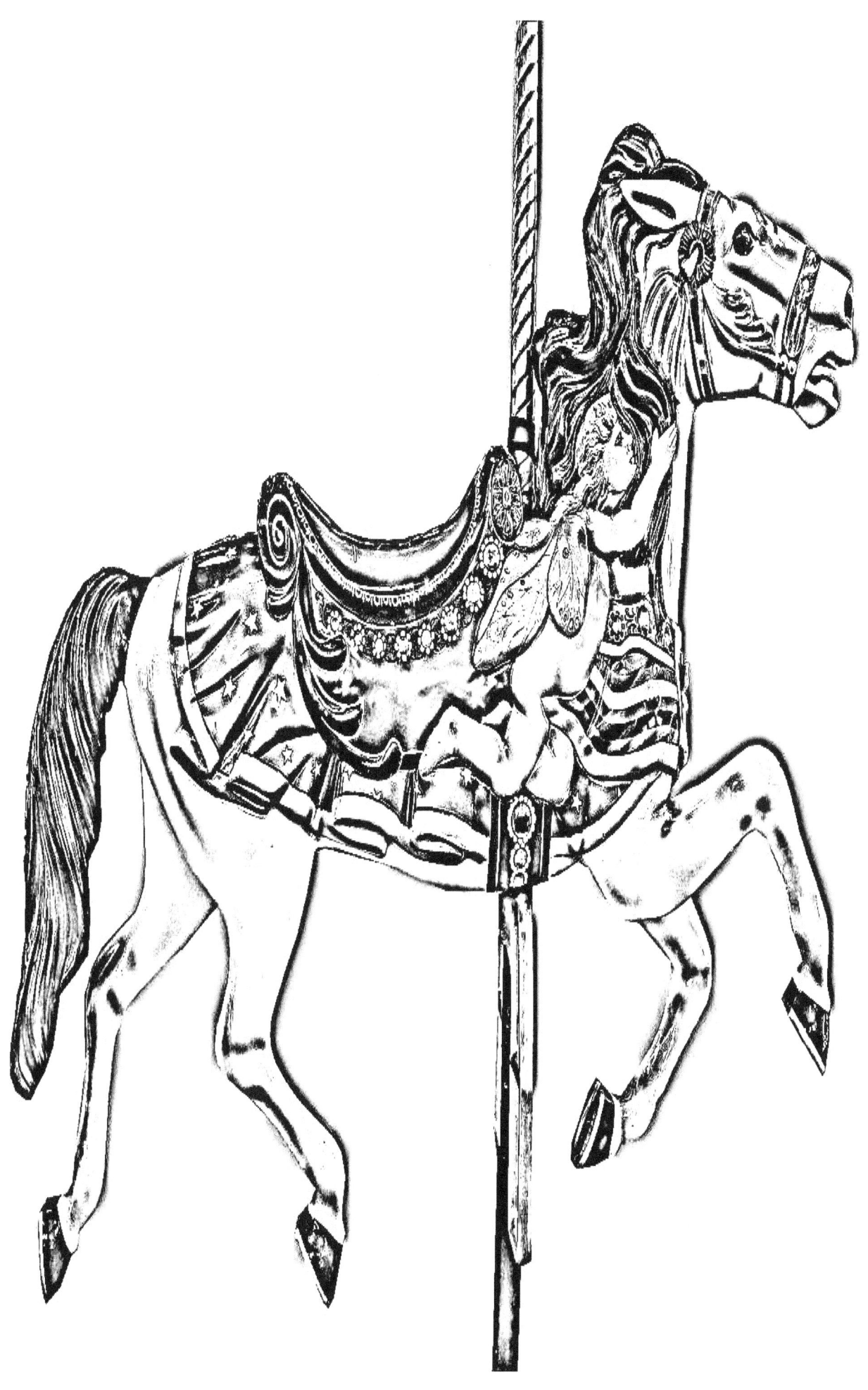

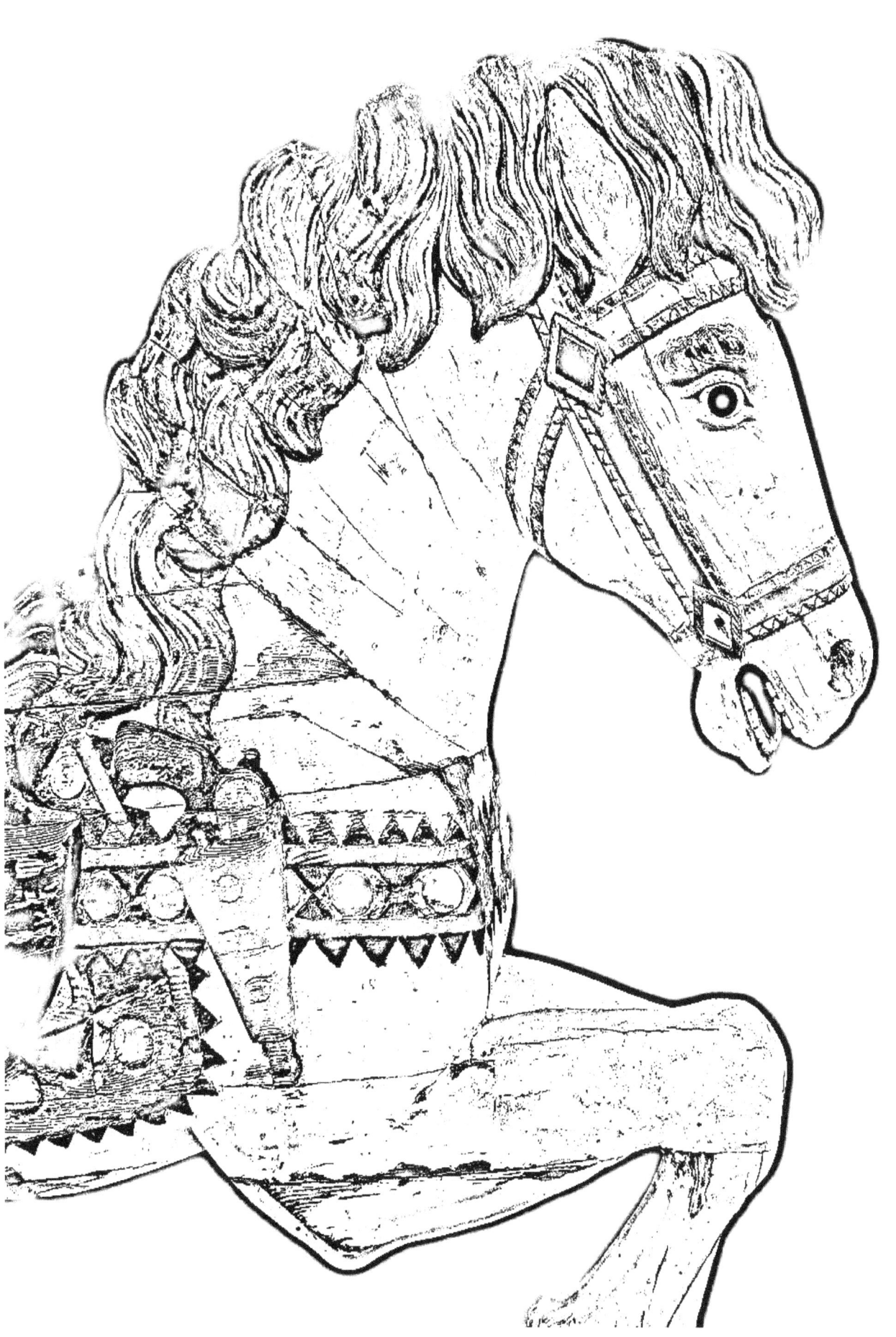

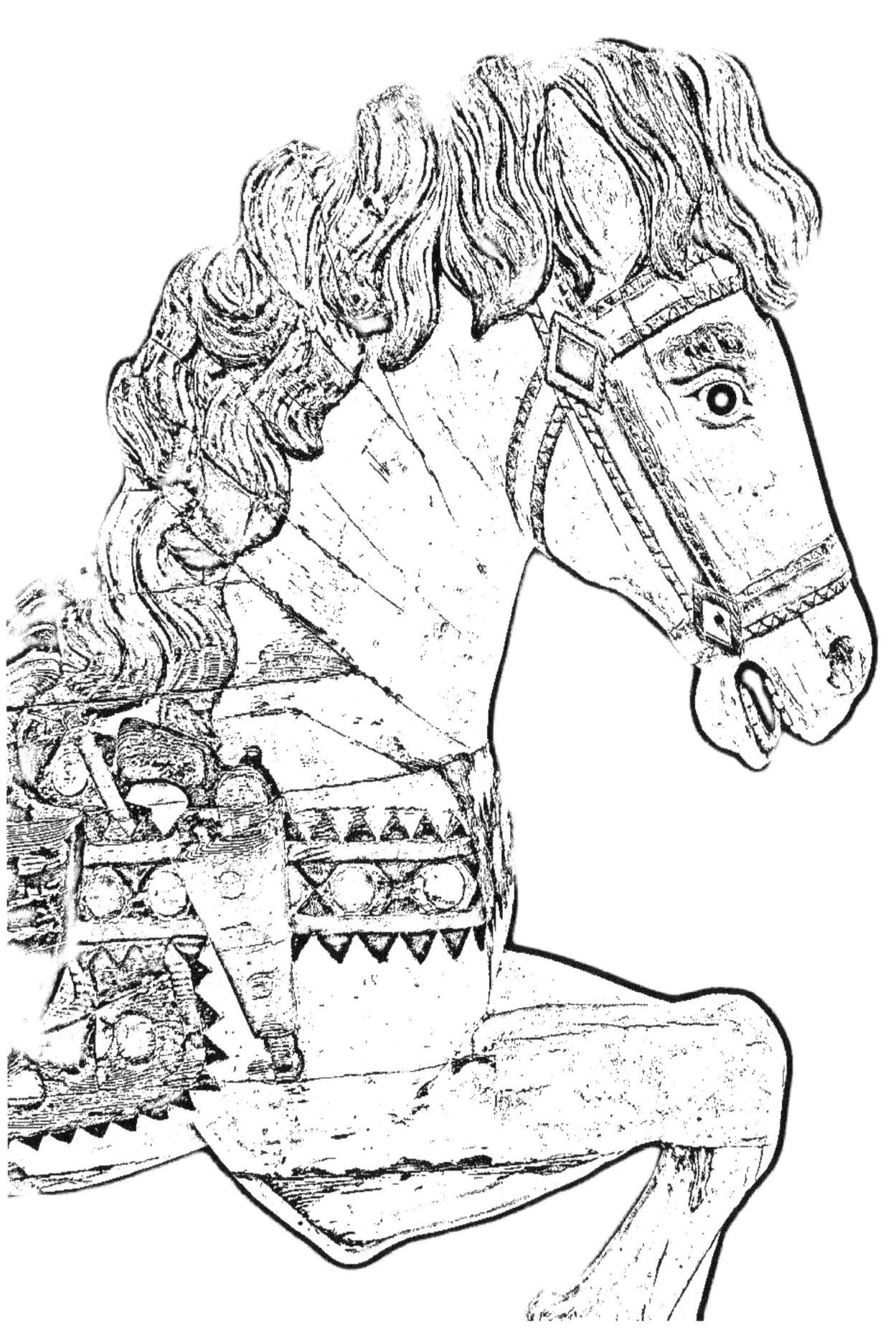

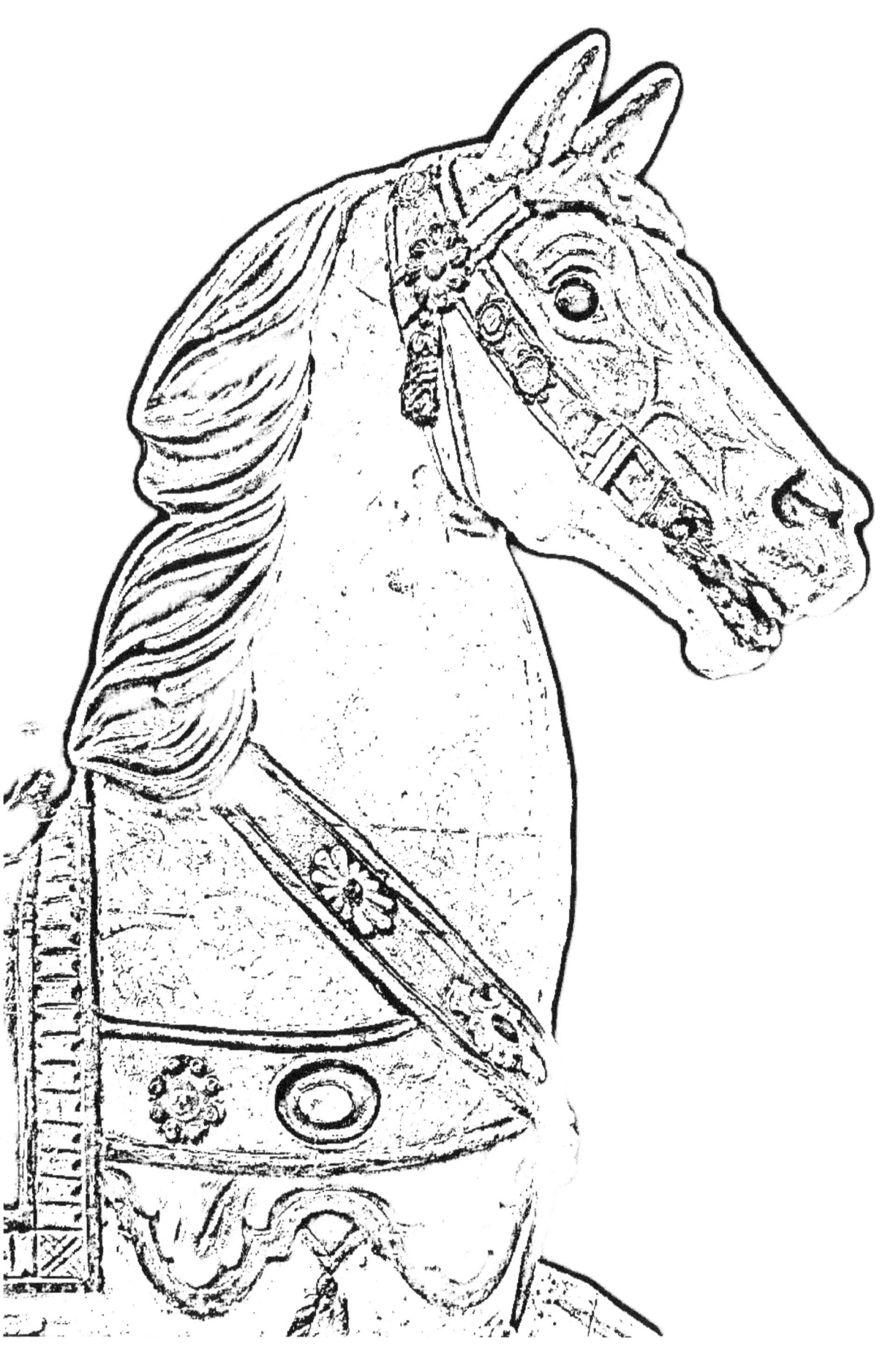

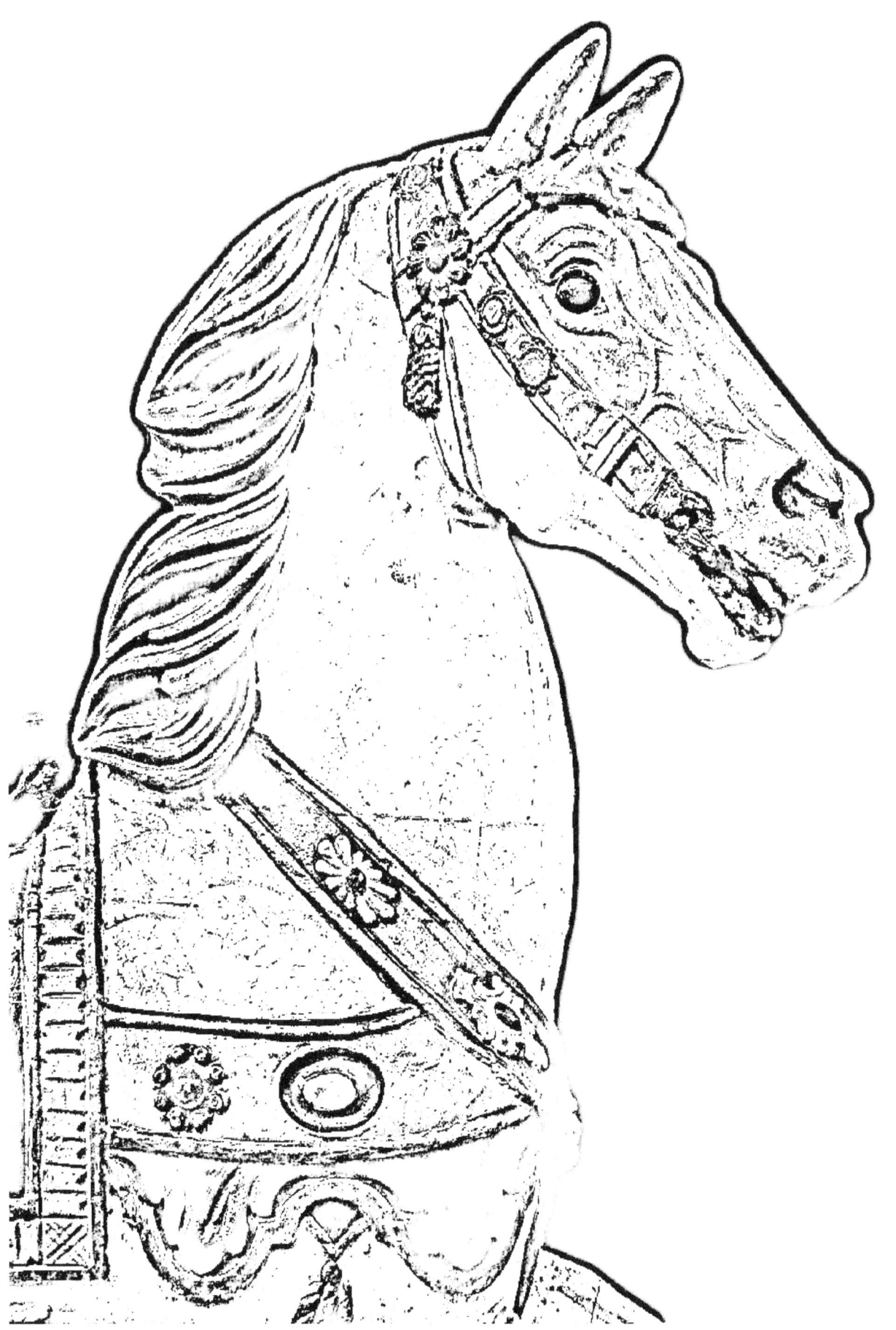

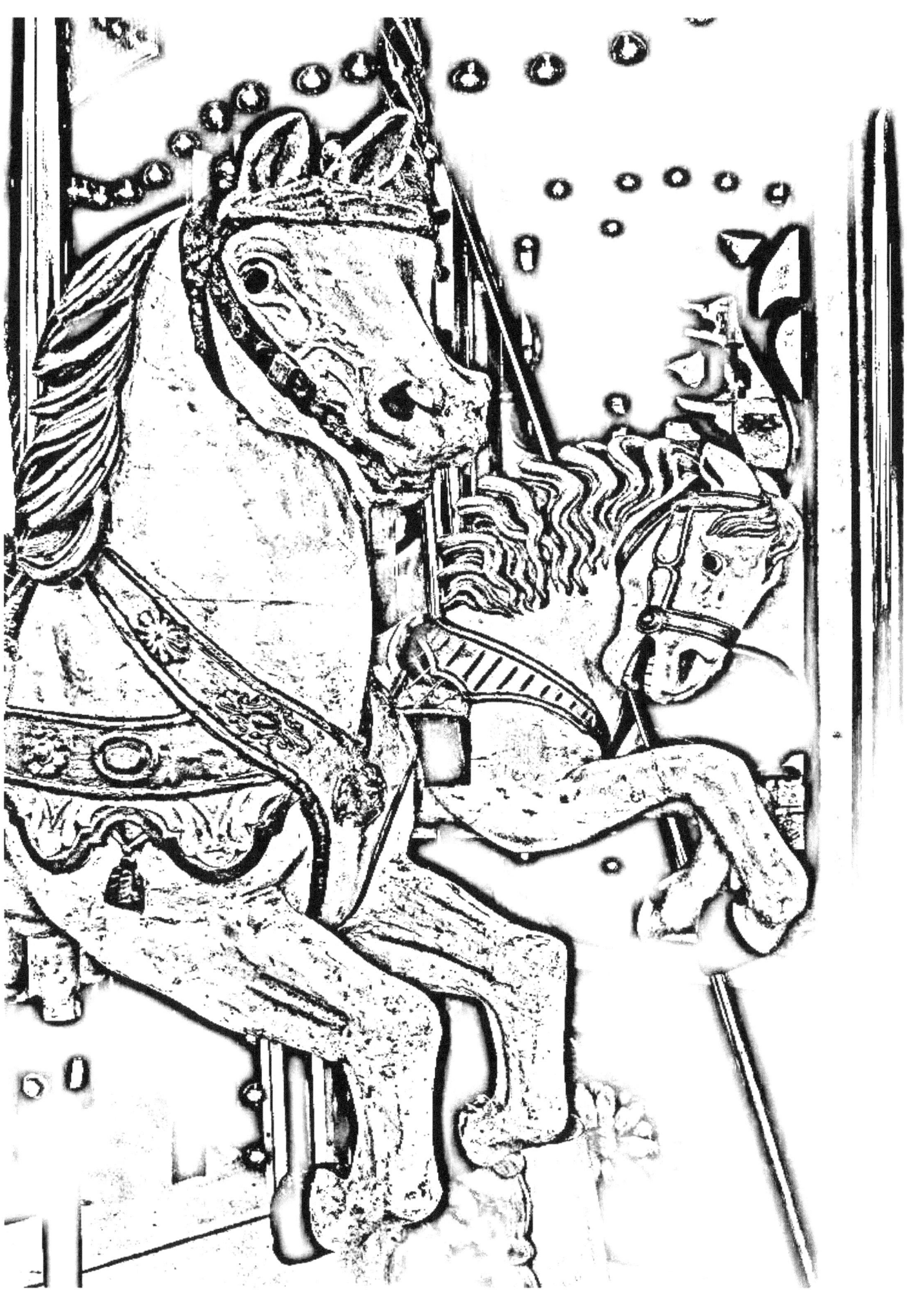

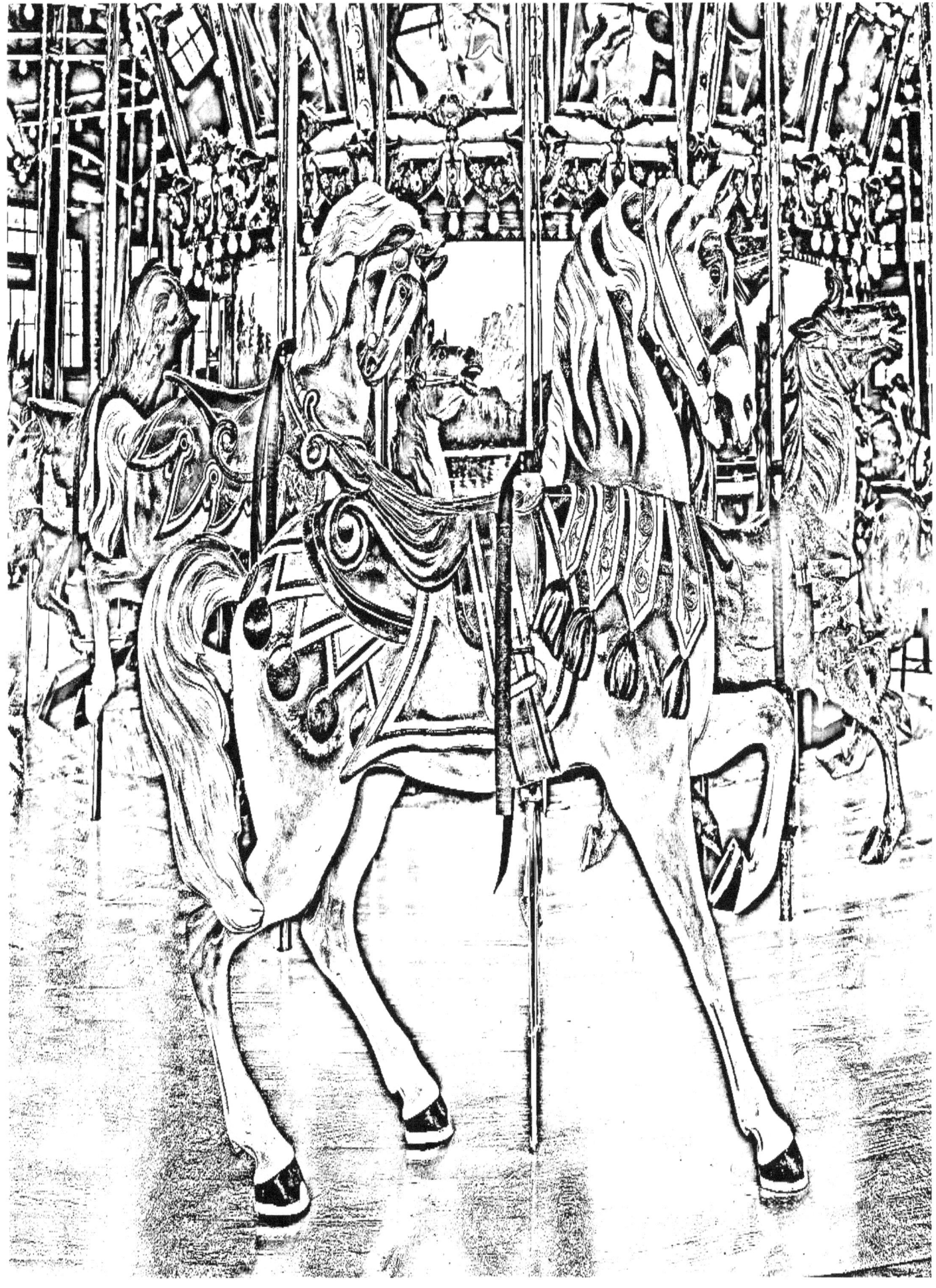

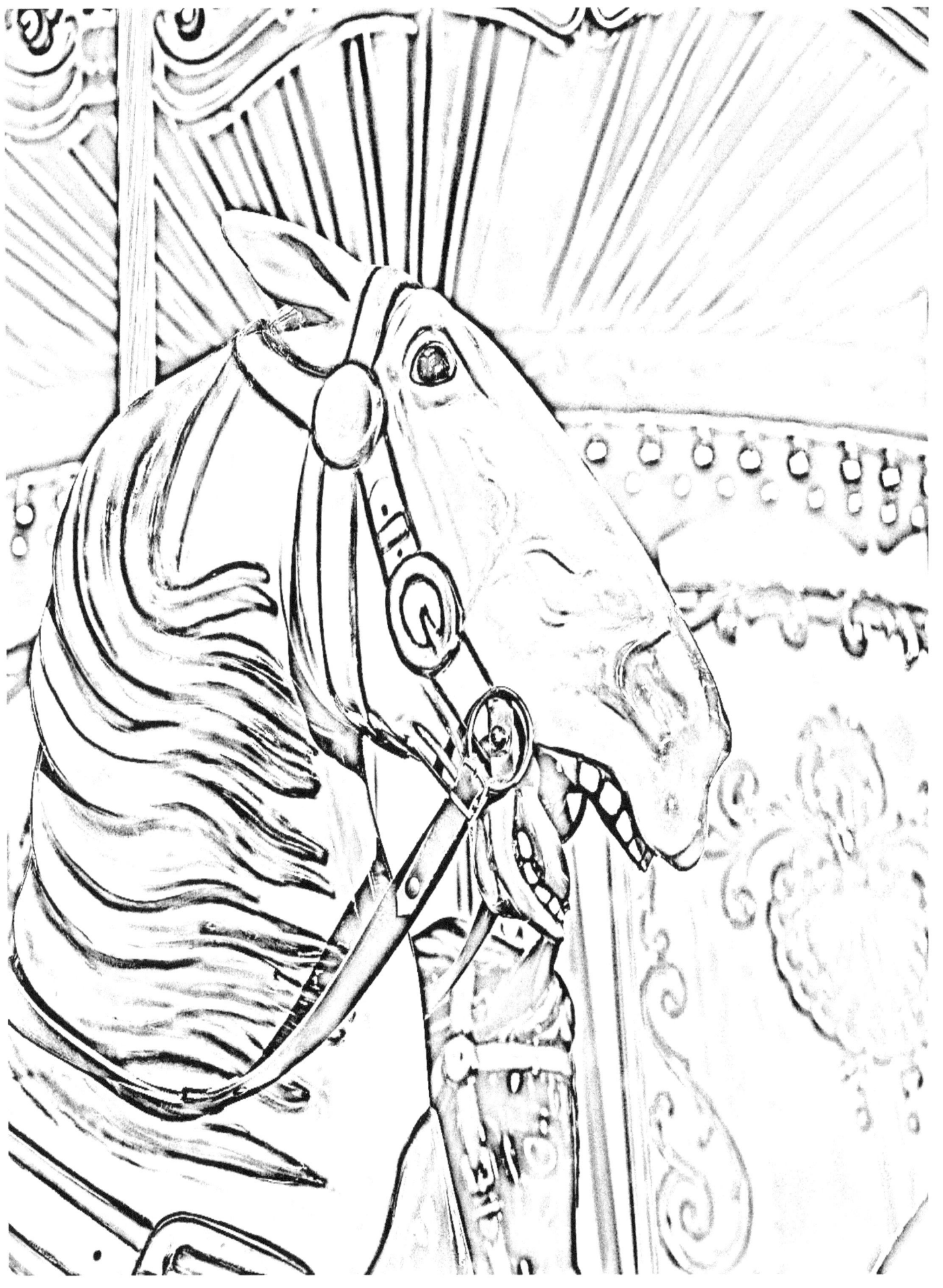

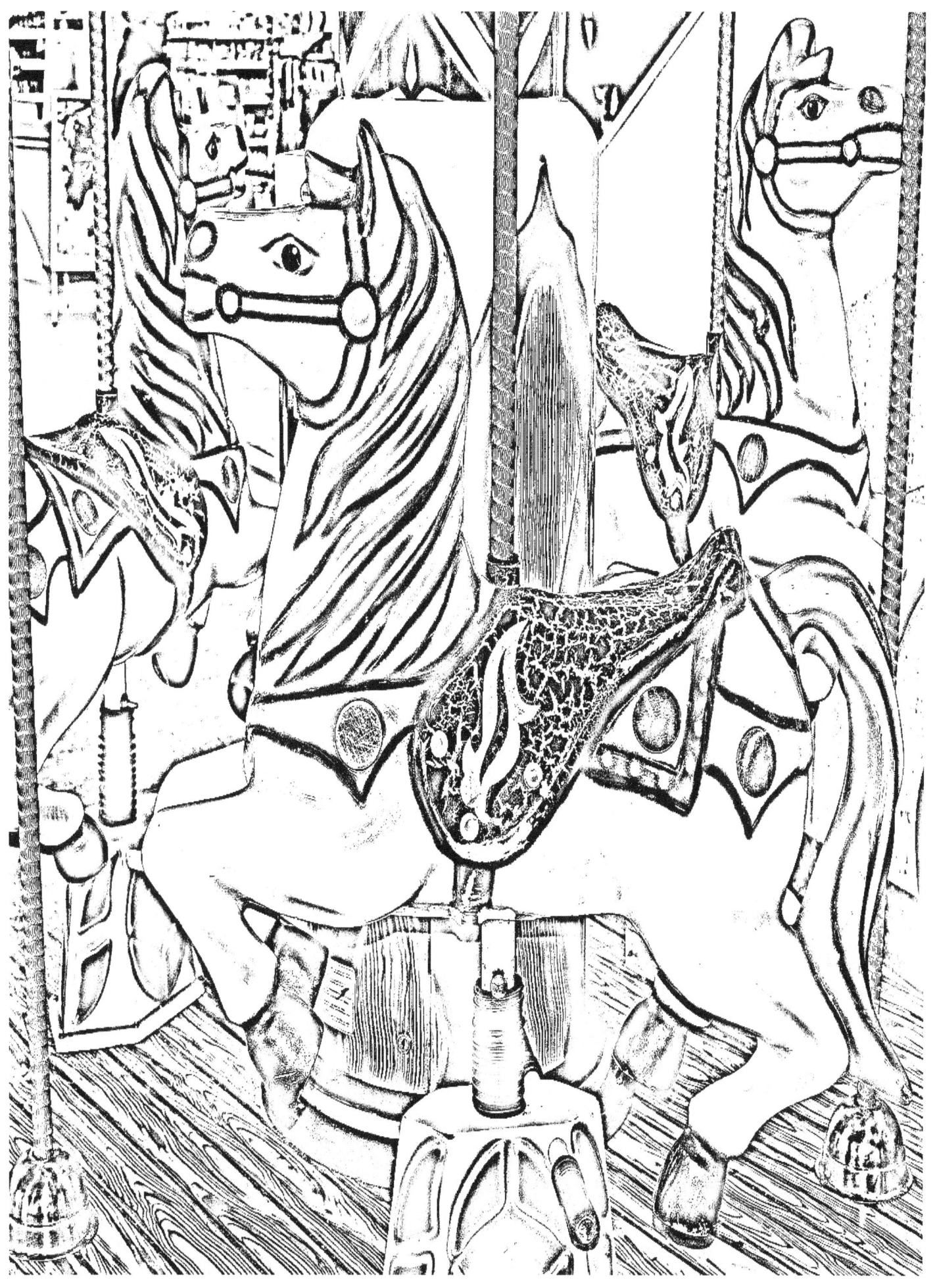

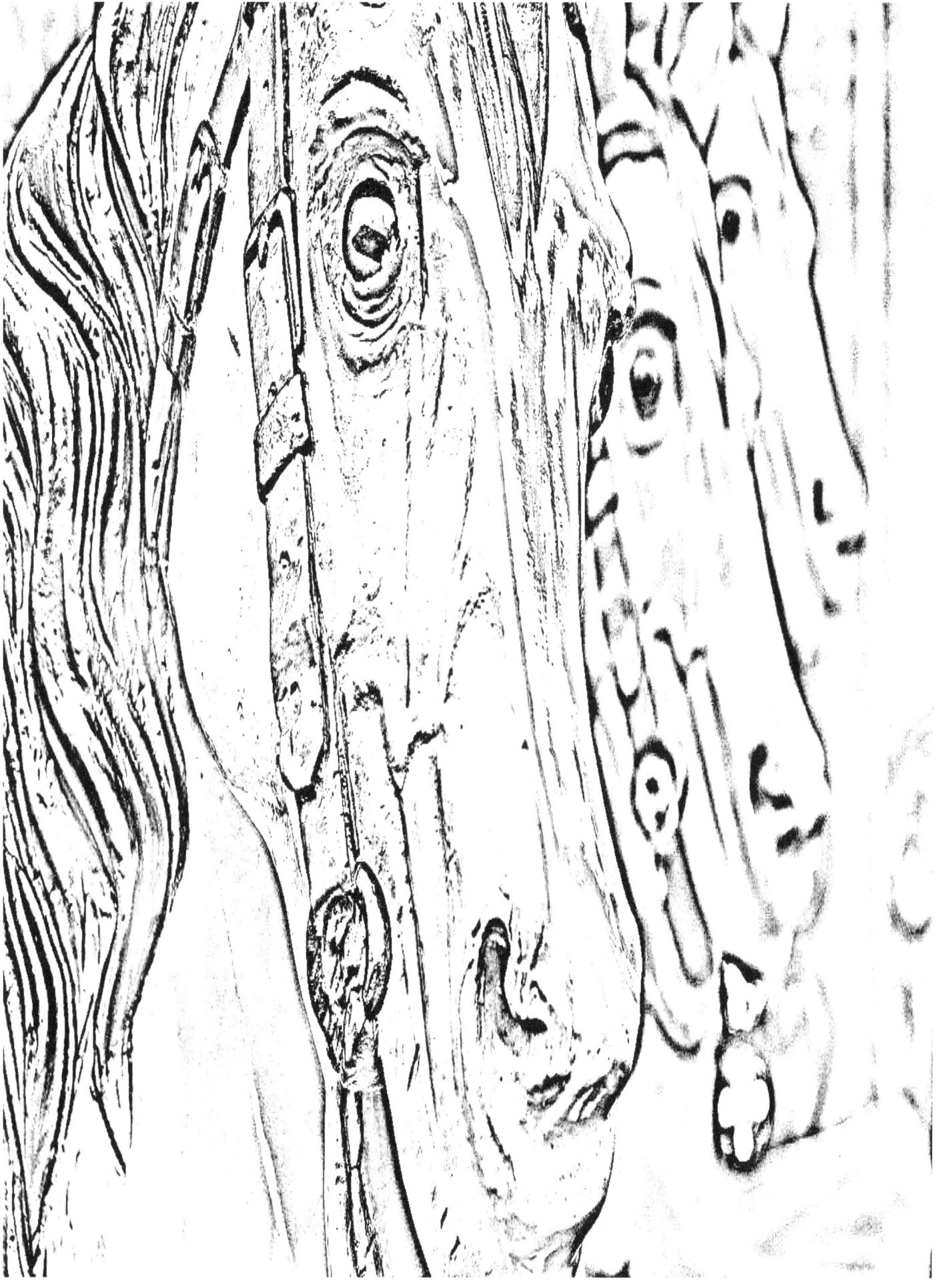

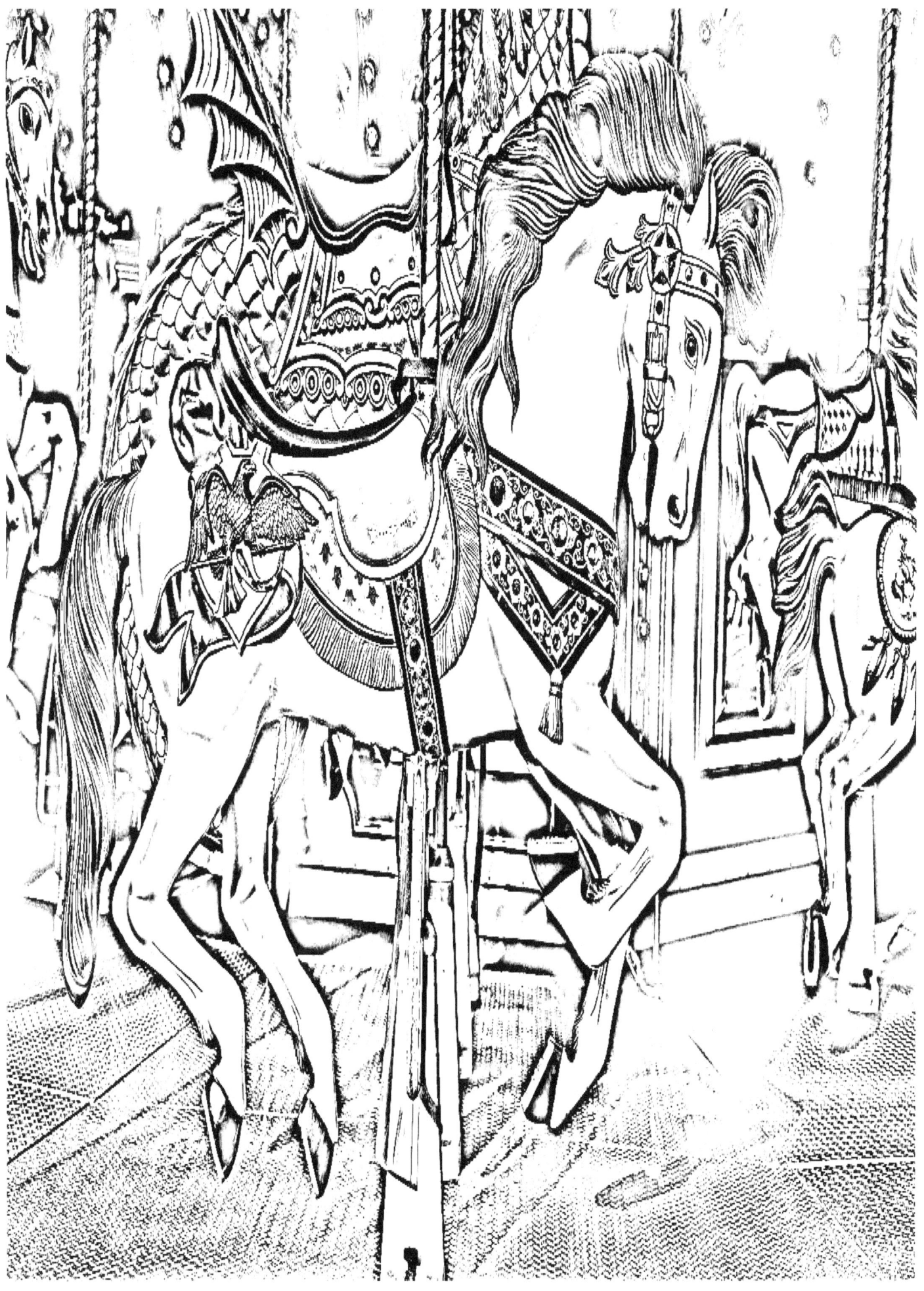

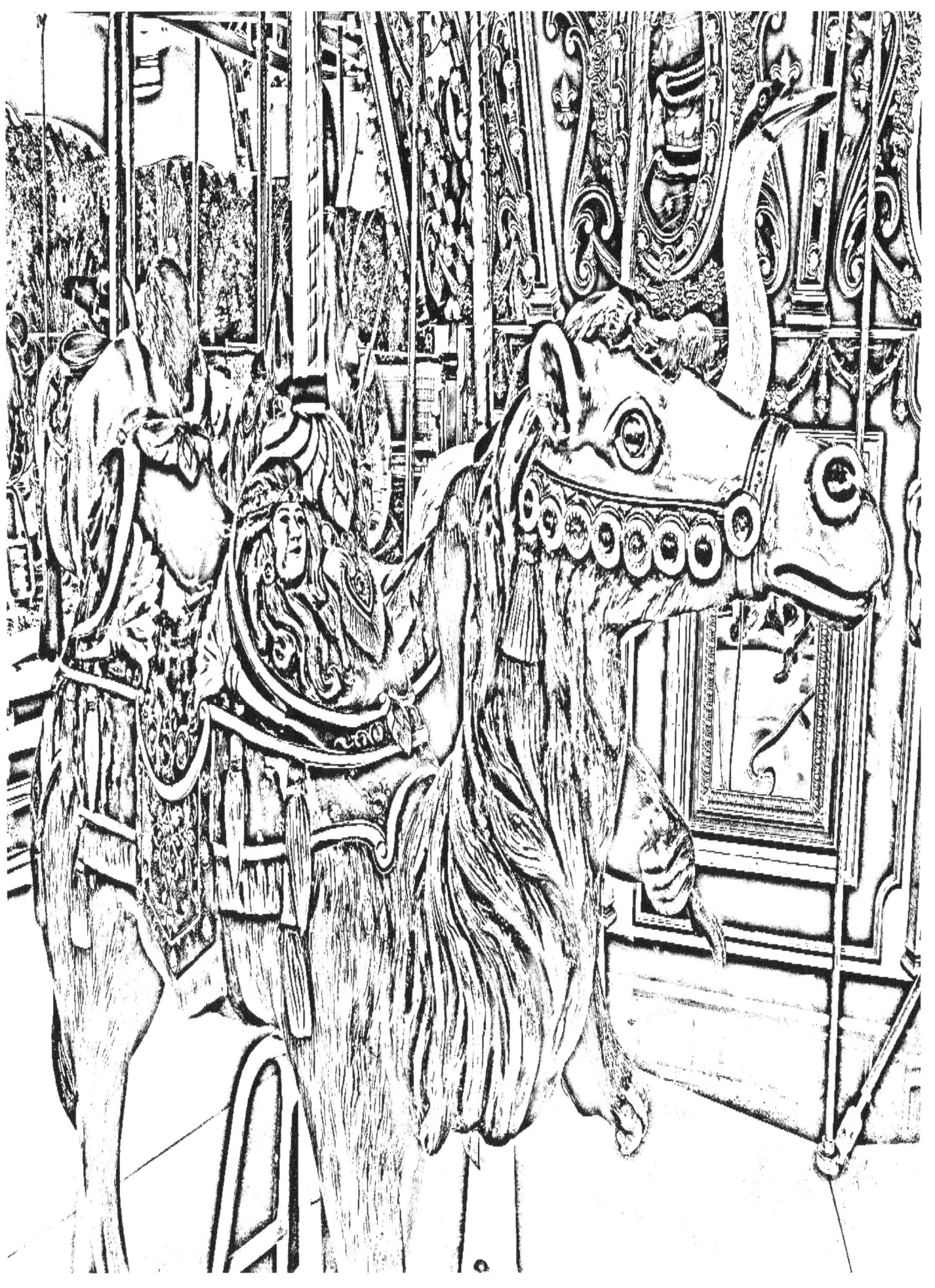

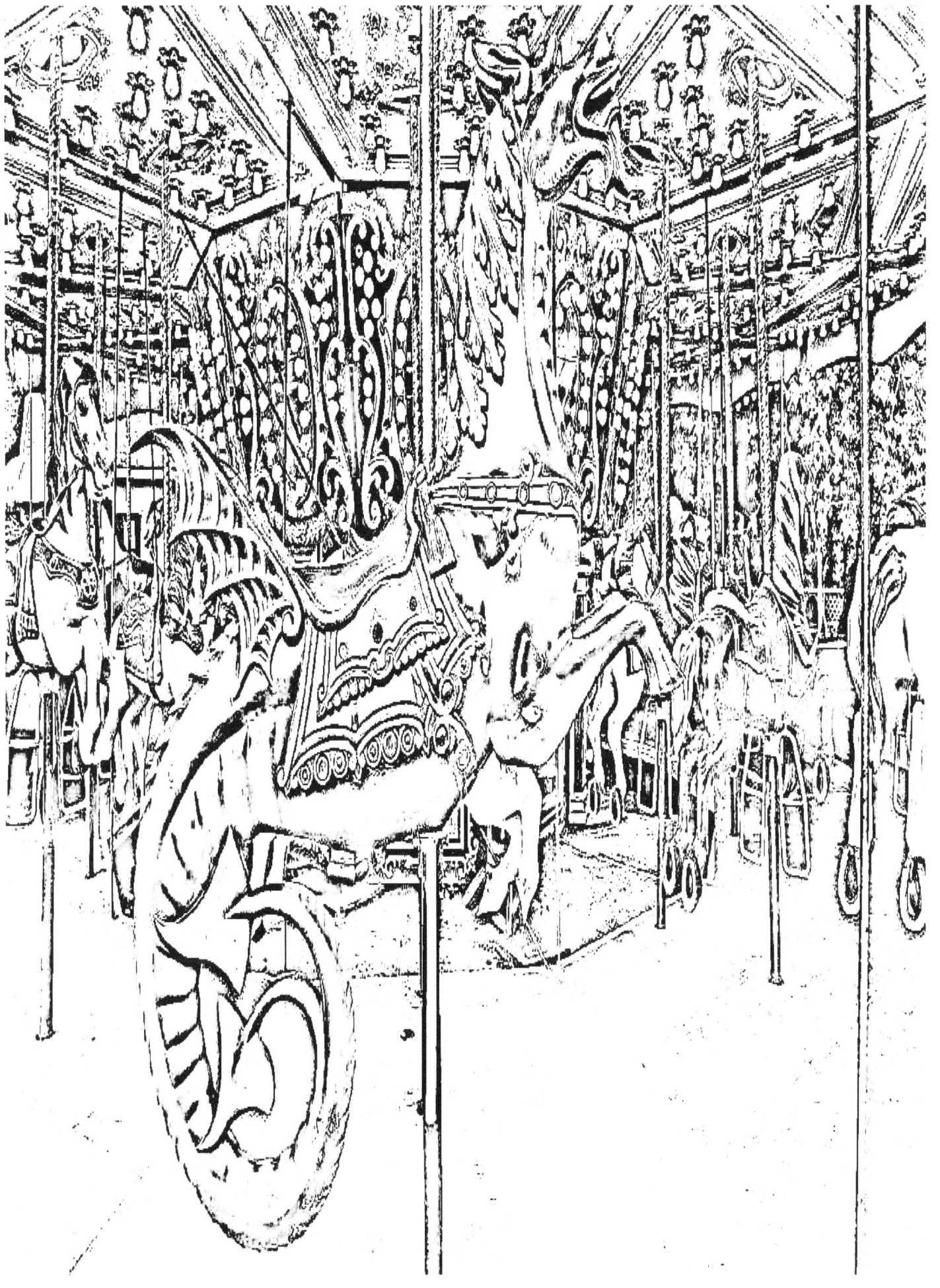

www.ingramcontent.com/pod-product-compliance
Lightning Source LLC
Chambersburg PA
CBHW080528190526
45169CB00008B/3091